Suffolk's Lost Railways
Neil Burgess

Ipswich Station, seen here on 5 July 1958, was opened by the Great Eastern Railway on 1 July 1860 and is still in use.

Capel Station.

Printed by
Blissetts, Roslin Road Acton, W3 8DH

The publishers regret that they cannot supply
copies of any pictures featured in this book.

Acknowledgements

I continue to be indebted to my friend and fellow railway historian Richard Morton for his meticulous proof reading and checking of the information
in this book. He has, as ever, drawn my attention to various points and inaccuracies and I am indebted to him for his diligence. The publishers wish to
thank the following for contributing photographs to this book: John Alsop for the front cover, pages 2, 11, 12, 14, 15, 16 (upper), 18, 19, 23, 24, 25, 29, 31,
32, 33, 34, 38, 39, 40, 41, 42, 44, 45, 47, and the back cover; and Richard Casserley for pages 4, 8, 9, 17, 20, 26, 27, 35, 43, 46, and 48.

INTRODUCTION

Over the last century and a half Suffolk has undergone considerable economic and social transformation. In the early part of the nineteenth century it was a landscape of predominantly mixed agriculture with some textile manufacturing and coastal fisheries. There were few towns of any size, principally Bury St Edmunds and Ipswich, and the majority of villages and market towns were small. Although it was relatively close to London, it seemed remarkably remote. By the middle of the twentieth century it had become a much more populous area, not least as a result of migration out of greater London, and a significant area for growing cereals and root crops, including sugar beet, as well as soft fruits. Although manufacturing industry was still poorly represented, some of the coastal ports had developed considerably and both Lowestoft and particularly Felixstowe had become significant gateways to the European mainland and beyond.

The railway age came slowly to Suffolk. The lack of significant centres of population meant that it was not a prime candidate for trunk lines and by the time railway building was well underway in the rest of England in the early 1840s Suffolk accounted for very little of the nation's route mileage. The mid-to-late 1840s saw the involvement of the famous – or notorious – George Hudson in the county's projected railways, but mainly because he hoped to use the Eastern Counties Railway to thwart the Great Northern Railway's proposed plans to connect London and York, which threatened his Midland Railway interests. After Hudson had been disgraced the Eastern Counties Railway grew in size, but also gained a well-deserved reputation for poor service and almost total disregard of its users' interests. Eventually, in 1862, it amalgamated with the Eastern Union and the East Suffolk companies to form the Great Eastern Railway. The GER had an almost complete monopoly of railways in East Anglia, but by the 1870s it was well on the way to establishing itself as a reliable and forward-thinking company which did a good deal to develop the economy of the region.

That economy was adversely affected by the great agricultural depression which began during the 1870s with the advent of large quantities of cheap imported grain from the vast prairies of Canada and the United States and later included equally cheaply imported refrigerated meat from Australasia and Latin America. East Anglian fisheries, particularly those in Yarmouth and Lowestoft, provided some diversification as did fruit growing and market gardening generally, the latter helped by rapid transit by train to major centres, including London; but British agriculture remained depressed right up to the outbreak of the Second World War in 1939. Poor returns led to a gradual migration from the countryside and many small towns and villages shrank in population right up to the 1950s. This last point was particularly paradoxical given the common Victorian preoccupation with railway building as a hedge against the decline of towns and villages. Not to have a railway was feared to be a first step towards inevitable oblivion, yet in Suffolk, as in some other rural counties, the railways probably aided and abetted the decline by encouraging the development of centres like Bury, Ipswich and Lowestoft at the expense of the villages and small towns. Some help was given to the countryside during the two world wars, the second seeing significant numbers of air stations created from which the RAF, and later the United States Army Air Force, could bomb the cities and industries of Germany.

Railway building in Suffolk was no easy matter. The stereotype of East Anglia as an unrelievedly flat landscape ignores many of the subtle problems which beset the railway promoters and civil engineers. One was that the coastline has a good many inlets which gave access to navigable rivers in the pre-railway age and beyond. These inlets were often wide and surrounded by greater expanses of marsh and mudflats, which proved difficult to cross. North-south railway links tended to be built some distance inland, which made them relatively remote from the existing small coastal towns and harbours, which then needed to be served by branch lines rather than direct main lines. Even inland the terrain was by no means easy since the north-to-south lines tended to keep intersecting with the river valleys, which flowed west-to-east. Add to this the central plateau which makes up much of East Anglia and the result was either a more-or-less direct route which undulated up hill and down dale, or else a route following the land contours which was more level, but considerably less direct. In the early railway age when speeds were low this was less of a problem than it often became later on, particularly in the years after the First World War when the railways began to feel the cold winds of competition from road transport which could not only serve communities more directly but which, in time, became faster than some of the secondary lines.

East Anglian railways could therefore be an interesting mixture of main lines, which the Great Eastern and its successor the London & North Eastern often operated with some panache, and rural byways which might, particularly in their latter days during the 1950s, look distinctly old-fashioned and quaint. Unsurprisingly, as this book will show, a number of the smaller branches lost their passenger services during the early 1950s or even before. Such closures included Suffolk's two most singular independent companies, the standard gauge Mid Suffolk Light Railway and the narrow gauge Southwold Railway, which both exemplified attempts to develop sparsely populated rural areas by lines running west to east across the lie of the major trunk routes. Had the Mid Suffolk's promoters had their way the two companies would have shared a junction with the East Suffolk line at Halesworth; but, as the section on that line relates, this never came to pass. Frustrating though such byways might have been to the travelling public and railway managers, railway enthusiasts loved them and several lines, including the Mid Suffolk Light and the Mildenhall branch, earned a place within their affections. Sadly, most closed before the preservation movement had developed sufficiently to retain them for the future.

Suffolk's railways included stations which sometimes offered examples of interesting or even notable architecture. Sancton Wood designed Bury St Edmunds, which in its early days included an overall roof to the platforms, while Needham Market and Stowmarket, both by Frederick Barnes, were also significant. After the 1860s the Great Eastern designed a number of small stations all over its system which reflected a distinct 'family likeness' which blended well into their settings throughout East Anglia. Even the wooden buildings on minor lines like the Mid Suffolk Light had a charm to them.

Through the Victorian age and particularly during the post-Second World War period, when paid holidays became a feature of life, Suffolk's coastal towns and villages often developed as seaside resorts and the railways cultivated this traffic, particularly in the years before car ownership mushroomed during the 1960s. Their capacity to move large numbers of people over long distances was undoubtedly a benefit to the resorts and their visitors alike, though the inevitable strains on the network of large numbers of people travelling over a relatively short season may have made many journeys seem longer and less comfortable than might have been wished. Sadly, even these sources of traffic could not save some lines which, outside of the season from mid-July to mid-September, tended to relapse into a slow, poorly patronised torpor which made them prime targets for rationalisation.

The Beeching Report, entitled *The Reshaping of British Railways* and published in 1963, sealed the fate of many of the surviving branch lines of Suffolk, but it was not all decay and despair. During the 1960s, under the tenure of Gerard Fiennes, probably one of the more inspired regional managers of the period, the East Suffolk line became a prototype of the concept of the 'basic railway', by which lines could

be made profitable by reducing facilities to a minimum while developing a more frequent and reliable train service using multiple-unit diesel trains for passengers and bulk loads for freight. More recently still, parts of the county's railway network, especially those serving Ipswich, have been electrified and Felixstowe grew beyond imagining by the development of roll-on-roll-off ferry and container transport, which is capable of transfer to freightliner trains – precisely the formula Beeching envisaged for future freight operations. The growth of population in those parts of the county linked easily to London has done much to develop the fortunes of Suffolk and its surviving railways and their place seems assured within the overall national network. The lines are arranged here in a north-to-south order.

Clare Station, on the Shelford–Haverhill –Sudbury line, 7 July 1956.

Snape Junction.

Snape Station.

The railway to Snape left the Ipswich–Beccles–Lowestoft line, between Wicham Market and Saxmundham, at Snape Junction and ran to its station at Snape Maltings about a mile distant. It was built in 1859 as one of Suffolk's few purpose-built goods lines by entrepreneur Newson Garrett and never carried passengers. The line was operated initially by the Eastern Counties Railway and services continued until its closure in the 1960s.

Yarmouth — Gorleston — Lowestoft *

Passenger service withdrawn	4 May 1970 (but see text)
Distance	12 ¾ miles
Company	Norfolk & Suffolk Joint Committee
	(Great Eastern and Midland & Great Northern Joint)

Stations closed	*Date of closure*
Corton	4 May 1970
Lowestoft North	4 May 1970

* Closed passengers stations on this line that were in Norfolk were Yarmouth Beach, Gorleston North, Gorleston-on-Sea, Gorleston Golf Links and Hopton-on-Sea.

Lowestoft is one of the natural harbours along the east coast, standing on the mouth of Oulton Broad, itself the end of a river system improved in the early nineteenth century to allow Norwich to have an outlet to the sea via the River Waveney. Yarmouth, around ten miles to the north, is another of the ports of East Anglia, but the rivers cutting deep into the coastline made rail access between the two a rather circuitous matter during the nineteenth century, the line going through Somerleyton and St Olaves and including the single-track St Olaves swing bridge over Oulton Broad. A new, much shorter, route opened on 13 July 1903 under the auspices of the Norfolk & Suffolk Joint Committee, an alliance forged after years of rivalry between the Great Eastern and the Midland & Great Northern Joint railways, the latter reaching Yarmouth Beach from the north. The line involved a reversal at Beach Station for traffic arriving in Yarmouth off the M&GNJ system, the line curving round through more than 180 degrees from Caister Road Junction, crossing over the Great Eastern line to Yarmouth fish market, striding across the outlet of Breydon Water on a swing bridge before crossing over the Great Eastern line into Yarmouth South Town. Just after this, at North Line Junction, it met the Great Eastern's connection from South Town to travel through Gorleston North, Hopton-on-Sea and Corton before joining the line from Haddiscoe at Coke Ovens Junction to run into Lowestoft Central. In fact, the M&GNJ owned the line from Beach to North Line Junction, the Joint Committee's section running from there to Coke Ovens.

Despite its convenience, the line was poorly patronised, even in the height of the summer holiday season. Most passengers arriving from the east midlands over the M&GNJ finished their journeys at Yarmouth rather than Lowestoft. Fish traffic was important before the 1930s but its decline could not be wholly offset by passengers in the summer. The three and a quarter-mile northern section from Yarmouth Beach to Gorleston was closed from 21 September 1953 when major repairs to the Breydon Viaduct and swing bridge became necessary; Yarmouth Beach closed along with the M&GNJ system on 2 March 1959. The remainder of the line eked out an existence throughout the 1960s, even surviving the Beeching closures, though goods services ended on 3 July 1967. The finale came with withdrawal of the paytrain service from 4 May 1970.

Tivetshall — Beccles *

Passenger service withdrawn   5 January 1953

Distance   19 ½ miles

Company   Waveney Valley Railway

* Closed passenger stations on this line that were in Norfolk were Tivetshall, Pulham Market, Pulham St Mary, Starston, Harleston, Redenhall, Wortwell, Homersfield, Earsham, Ditchingham, Ellingham and Gledestron.

Stations closed	Date of closure
Bungay	5 January 1953

Bungay Station.

In the 1840s travellers wishing to go from Yarmouth, Lowestoft, Bungay or Beccles to London needed to follow a rather roundabout route taking in Norwich and Cambridge. A more direct alternative was planned along the Waveney Valley, but it was never built. The people of Harleston therefore promoted a line of their own from Tivetshall, on the Ipswich–Norwich line of the Eastern Counties Railway. Opened under the title of the Waveney Valley Railway in 1855, the line was subsequently extended eastwards to Bungay in 1860 and Beccles in 1863, where it made a connection with the East Suffolk line. The Eastern Counties had originally worked the line, but in its last two years of independent existence – it was merged with the Great Eastern on the day it was opened to Beccles - it was worked by the owning company.

The line was mostly in Norfolk, only entering Suffolk around Bungay where the county boundary loops northwards to create almost an island into Norfolk. There was little likelihood of extensive local traffic and no significant towns along the route so it was an easy candidate for closure, which came to passengers in January 1953. Goods services retreated more gradually, the Harleston–Bungay section closing entirely from 1 February 1960, Bungay–Ditchingham from 3 August 1964, and Beccles–Ditchingham from 19 April 1965. The final section to succumb was the original line between Tivetshall and Harleston which closed from 18 April 1966, 111 years after first opening.

Mellis — Eye

Passenger service withdrawn	2 February 1931	*Stations closed*	*Date of closure*
Distance	3 miles	Yaxley Halt	2 February 1931
Company	Mellis & Eye Railway	Eye	2 February 1931

Eye Station.

The fear of being consigned to a long, gradual decline due to the Eastern Counties Railway passing three miles away led to the inhabitants of Eye, a once-prosperous market town, promoting their own railway to connect with the main line at Mellis. The independence of the line was circumscribed by the Great Eastern undertaking to operate it from its opening on 2 April 1867, the little company being wholly absorbed by its neighbour in 1898. The railway was unable to stem Eye's decline and the passenger service was another of those which felt the force of road competition after the First World War. One of the Great Eastern's final acts was to open a halt at Yaxley in December 1922, but it was unavailing and the passenger service ceased from 1931. Coal and sugar beet provided sufficient goods traffic up to the early 1960s but this was not enough to keep the line alive and it finally closed completely from 13 July 1964.

Fordham — Mildenhall *

Passenger service withdrawn	18 June 1962
Distance	7 ¼ miles
Company	Great Eastern Railway

* Closed passenger station on this line that were in Cambridgeshire were Fordham and Isleham.
** Opened in 1922 as Mildenhall Golf Links Halt and renamed in 1923.

Stations closed	*Date of closure*
Worlington Golf Links Halt **	18 June 1962
Mildenhall	18 June 1962

Worlington Golf Links Halt, 1953.

The branch line to Mildenhall was in effect two branches, having a total length of 20¾ miles, but built in two sections and running through two counties. The first section, between Cambridge and Fordham, on the line between Bury St Edmunds and Ely, opened on 2 June 1884 with the seven and a quarter mile section thence to Mildenhall on 1 April the following year. Mildenhall was a market town which for most of the line's existence was a small centre adjoining the fens, so the potential traffic was fairly sparse. The change came with the Second World War when the United States Army Air Force established a large bomber station near the town, which added to the traffic, though in the end not enough to keep the line in existence.

Operation of the line was something of a paradox. For most of the time a push-pull train, introduced in 1913, was more than adequate; but on market days a tender engine and more coaches were needed and the push-pull engine could not manage mixed trains – conveying both passenger coaches and goods wagons – which would have sufficed if traffic was less than usual. The solution was to employ the Holden 'Intermediate' 2-4-0 tender engines (LNER class E4) on trains of ancient coaches, services usually running through to and from Cambridge. The line proved to be one of the last duties of the class, including British Railways No. 62785, now preserved under its former identity as Great Eastern No. 490 as part of the National Railway Museum's collection. The infrequent service on the line made it ideal for railway enthusiasts' excursions during the 1950s and it became far better known than its length and location might have suggested; from time to time Cambridge University Railway Society would hire an E4 and train for trips over the branch on Saturdays and students could even try their hand at driving the engine, a facility probably unique in the history of excursions. The E4s gave way to diesel railbuses in 1958, but these were insufficient to secure the line's future and it closed to passengers on 18 June 1962, goods services to Mildenhall ending two years later.

Thetford — Bury St Edmunds *

Passenger service withdrawn	8 June 1953	*Stations closed*	*Date of closure*
Distance	12 ¾ miles	Seven Hills Halt	8 June 1953
Company	Bury St Edmunds & Thetford Railway	Ingham	8 June 1953

Stations closed	*Date of closure*	* The closed passenger station on this line that was in Norfolk was Thetford
Barnham	8 June 1953	Bridge.

Barnham Station.

Ingham Station.

Bury St Edmunds was and is one of the principal towns in Suffolk and one which benefited from the greater mobility afforded by the coming of railways. The line northwards to Thetford, across the county boundary in Norfolk, was one of the last to be constructed from Bury, being incorporated in 1865. Raising capital proved difficult for the nominally independent company and it entered into an alliance with the Thetford & Watton Railway, with which it made an end-on connection. Only on 1 March 1876 did the Bury line open to goods traffic, passenger being carried from 15 November. The T&WR actually worked the Bury line from its opening and laid in a connection at Thetford Bridge to allow through running. Two years later, the B&T gladly accepted the Great Eastern's offer of purchase, the T&WR and its northern neighbour, the Watton & Swaffham Railway, entering the same fold the following year. The Thetford Bridge spur was closed from 1880 and the companies were all formally absorbed into the Great Eastern in 1898. The end of through running from Swaffham consigned the Thetford–Bury line to secondary status, reinforced by weight and speed restrictions.

The line came into its own mainly during the two world wars. Barnham hosted a large military stores depot in both conflicts while the latter war saw a chemical works constructed on the Bury side of the station, along with a vast bomb dump for the RAF. The return of peace in 1945 left the line with little revenue and passenger services ended from 8 June 1953, goods continuing for only a further seven years until 27 June 1960.

Southwold — Halesworth

		Stations closed	Date of closure
Passenger service withdrawn	12 April 1929	Southwold	12 April 1929
Distance	8 ¾ miles	Walberswick	12 April 1929
Company	Southwold Railway	Blythburgh	12 April 1929
		Wenhaston	12 April 1929

Southwold Station, *c.*1910.

Walberswick Station.

If it was felt essential for an area to be served by a railway for it to have any chance of economic development, there were sometimes difficulties in deciding exactly what sort of railway was required. The more marginal the area, the greater the need for an inexpensive line, eschewing large civil engineering works and extensive facilities. The concept of the light railway was eventually enshrined in law by the Light Railways Act of 1896, but long before this date a variety of lightly constructed lines had appeared. In addition to the surviving Welsh narrow gauge lines (now operated as heritage railways), there grew up an extensive network of three-foot gauge lines in the more remote parts of Ireland. In England, though, the narrow gauge was a decided rarity and eastern England boasted only one, constructed from Halesworth on the East Suffolk line to the small port of Southwold. Incorporated in 1876 – only thirteen years after the Ffestiniog Railway had pioneered the use of steam traction on the narrow gauge – the Southwold Railway opened on 24 September 1879.

Blythburgh Station, c.1909.

Up to the outbreak of war in 1914 the railway certainly played a part in stimulating the economy of Southwold and its hinterland, both as a working port and as a tourist destination. However, the Southwold's indifference to the discipline of the timetable was legendary and the post-1918 world of rising costs and faster, more convenient road transport – coupled with the dominance of Lowestoft over Southwold as a port – placed intolerable burdens on the small company. Even so, the refusal of its directors to consider selling out to the Great Eastern in 1893 and the London & North Eastern in 1923 can only be seen retrospectively as recklessness; an eleventh-hour change of heart which led to attempts to persuade the LNER to take over the line in 1929 came too late and the line closed completely on 12 April that year. The locomotives and rolling stock, which included some of the very few examples of narrow gauge private owners' coal wagons, owned by Moy's of Colchester, quietly rusted and rotted away until being gathered up in the wartime scrap drive of 1941/42.

Haughley — Laxfield

Passenger service withdrawn	27 July 1952
Distance	21 ¼ miles
	(plus 2 ½ miles from Kenton to near Debenham - see text)
Company	Mid Suffolk Light Railway

Stations closed	*Date of closure*
Haughley East *	January 1925
Mendlesham	28 July 1952
Brockford & Wetheringsett	28 July 1952
Aspall & Thorndon	28 July 1952

Stations closed	*Date of closure*
Kenton	28 July 1952
Worlingworth	28 July 1952
Horham	28 July 1952
Stradbroke	28 July 1952
Wilby	28 July 1952
Laxfield	28 July 1952

Note: some sources give the closure dates as 28 July 1952.
* Originally named Haughley until 1 July 1923.

Mid Suffolk Light Railway locomotive No. 2 at Haughley Station in 1905, when the buildings were still under construction.

The Southwold Railway was conceived and built two decades before the Light Railways Act of 1896, but the Mid Suffolk Light Railway was a product of that legislation, authorised by a Light Railway Order of 1901. The original intention was to construct a link between the north south routes linking Ipswich and Norwich to the west and the East Suffolk line to the east, providing a standard gauge light railway 28 miles long. In the event the line ran from Haughley on the Ipswich–Norwich line to Laxfield, a distance of 19 miles, the completion of the route to Halesworth being found impracticable due to marshland. This handicapped the MSLR from the outset, not helped by Suffolk County Council refusing to make a loan to assist construction. Delays meant the first goods service to Laxfield ran on 20 September 1904, while passenger services had to wait until 29 September 1908, not least because of the need to improve the line to carry passenger trains.

Mendlesham Station.

Aspall & Thorndon Station.

Locomotive No. 65447 at Kenton with the 1.45 p.m. service from Laxfield to Haughley, 16 April 1952.

In the meantime two attempts were made to find alternative routes from Laxfield to Halesworth, resulting in an extension west of the former of just two and a quarter miles to Cratfield, completed in 1906. A two and half mile branch from Kenton towards Debenham was constructed, but appears never to have seen regular services. The MSLR did truly live up to its image of a railway passing through the middle of nowhere to end in a field.

Mid Suffolk Light Railway locomotive No. 2 approaching Stradbroke Station with a Laxfield train, *c*.1911.

Like the Southwold and many other minor lines, the MSLR just about managed to break even before the First World War, but post-war economic stringency proved too much. Unlike its narrow-gauge neighbour – with which, had things gone to plan, it would have made an end-on connection at Halesworth – it was absorbed into the LNER at the 1923 Grouping. The Cratfield extension had gone after 1916, though for many years a spur of it remained beyond Laxfield, and the line struggled on through the Second World War, during which there was a short period of revival due to an aerodrome near Mendlesham.

The end eventually came under British Railways from 27 July 1952, though the line survived long enough to attract the attention of enthusiasts who discovered that the staff were more than willing to allow unofficial riding on goods trains and locomotives when officialdom was looking elsewhere.

Bury St Edmunds — Long Melford

Passenger service withdrawn	10 April 1961
Distance	16 ½ miles
Company	Eastern Counties Railway (but see text)

Stations closed	*Date of closure*
Welnetham	10 April 1961
Cockfield	10 April 1961
Lavenham	10 April 1961

Cockfield Station, 1953.

This line was originally proposed by the Eastern Counties Railway in 1861 as a link between the lines from Bury to Ipswich and Cambridge to Colchester. The ECR was absorbed into the Great Eastern in 1862 and that company promoted a new act for the line in the same year. It opened from 9 August 1865, single track throughout, and for most of its existence was a purely local route, though in later years it saw occasional through trains from the east midlands to seaside destinations like Clacton.

In 1959 passenger services were handed over to diesel multiple units in the hope of effecting economies, but these were not enough to keep it going and closure to passengers followed from 10 April 1961. The track between Lavenham and Long Melford was lifted in the following year, but services continued from Bury to Lavenham until 19 April 1965 when they also succumbed.

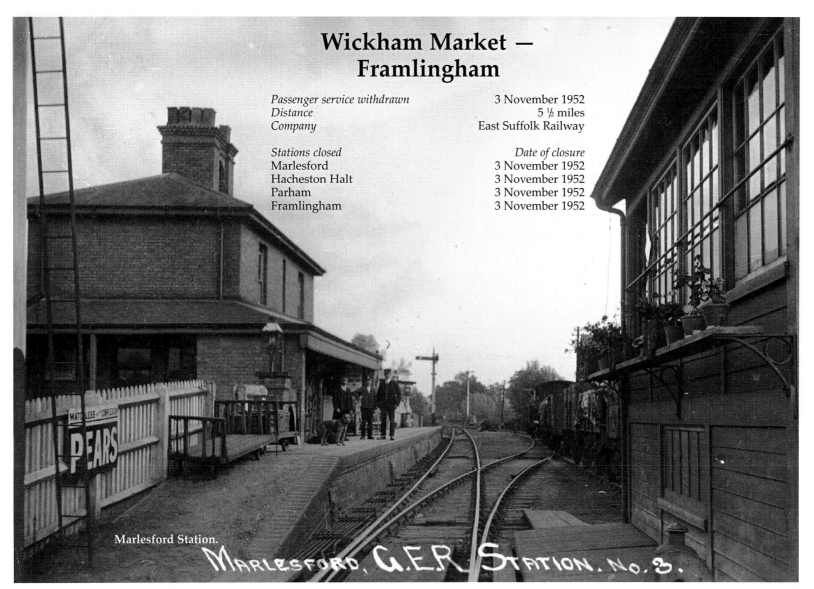

Wickham Market — Framlingham

Passenger service withdrawn	3 November 1952
Distance	5 ½ miles
Company	East Suffolk Railway

Stations closed	*Date of closure*
Marlesford	3 November 1952
Hacheston Halt	3 November 1952
Parham	3 November 1952
Framlingham	3 November 1952

Marlesford Station.

MARLESFORD. G.E.R. STATION. No. 3.

Parham Station, *c.*1908.

SMITHS

A further branch off the East Suffolk line connected Wickham Market to the small town of Framlingham, opened on 1 June 1859. The terminus was hardly very convenient for the town and the line was another which felt the cold blast of road competition for passengers early on. The LNER opened a halt at Hacheston in 1923, but eventually the line's passenger service, which had fluctuated between five and six return journeys a day, succumbed in 1952. Between the wars a sugar beet factory had been built at Framlingham and this, along with the town's granaries, kept the daily goods service going until 15 April 1965 when it, too, ended.

Saxmundham — Aldeburgh

Passenger service withdrawn	12 September 1966	*Stations closed*		*Date of closure*
Distance	4 miles	Leiston		12 September 1966
Company	East Suffolk Railway	Thorpeness		12 September 1966
		Aldeburgh *		12 September 1966

* Spelt as 'Aldborough' until 1875.

Leiston Station.

Leiston Station, 15 May 1956.

Although farming was the principal industry in nineteenth-century Suffolk, engineering also thrived, especially in the supply of machinery for agriculture. One renowned firm of engineers was Garrett's of Leiston, dating from 1778, whose owner during the 1850s, Richard Garrett, was a director of the East Suffolk Railway. Given the importance of Garrett's works it is hardly surprising that the ESR constructed a short branch from its main line at Saxmundham to Leiston, which opened on 1 June 1859. In the same year parliamentary authorisation was given to extend the line to Aldeburgh, a small fishing port which was also developing as a fashionable seaside resort, and the extension opened on 12 April 1860.

Saxmundham — Aldeburgh

Thorpeness Station, 14 May 1956.

Aldeburgh's fishing trade was helped by the line, large quantities of sprats and other fish being sent by train daily, but towards the end of the century the harbour became increasingly silted and the trade declined. The town's popularity as a resort continued, but it never became a large holiday centre despite the efforts of both the Great Eastern and London & North Eastern companies, which served the line with through coaches until the outbreak of the Second World War. After the war, in 1948, the composer Benjamin Britten, who lived in the town, founded the annual music festival with his friends Peter Pears and Eric Crozier, but despite its international reputation it was hardly sufficient to generate the traffic required to keep the line in operation. Attempts to develop Thorpeness as a resort were likewise unable to sustain passenger services and these ended in 1966, general goods services beyond Leiston having ceased from 30 November 1959.

Aldeburgh Station.

What has kept the line in existence, albeit foreshortened, was the decision of the Central Electricity Generating Board in 1960 to construct a new nuclear power station at Sizewell, between Leiston and Thorpeness. Between 1988 and 1995 a second nuclear power station, Sizewell 'B', was constructed alongside the original plant, now named Sizewell 'A'. Garrett's works, which for many years employed a curious steam locomotive named *Serapite*, built by Aveling & Porter, better known for their traction engines and road rollers, continued to provide traffic until 7 May 1984, but after that date the only regular workings on the line have been for the transportation of spent nuclear fuel to the reprocessing plant at Sellafield in Cumbria.

Bentley — Hadleigh

Passenger service withdrawn	29 February 1932	*Stations closed*	*Date of closure*
Distance	7 ¼ miles	Bentley	7 November 1966
Company	Eastern Union & Hadleigh Junction Railway	Capel	29 February 1932
		Raydon Wood	29 February 1932
		Hadleigh	29 February 1932

Bentley Station, *c.*1914.

The short branch off the East Suffolk line from Bentley to Hadleigh was one of those railways originally promoted as the beginning of a possible route going much further but which, in the event, was never built. Thus, the Eastern Union Railway, keen to prevent the rival Eastern Counties Railway from constructing a route from Ipswich to Norwich, promoted the nominally independent Eastern Union & Hadleigh Junction Railway as far as Hadleigh, with the prospect of an extension to Lavenham. Opened to goods on 21 August 1847 and to passengers on 2 September, the route was planned for double track but only a single line was ever laid. The EUR absorbed the company in the following year and it thereby passed into Great Eastern ownership in 1862, by which time all prospect of an extension had been forgotten.

Hadleigh Station, 1953.

The line was served by only around five return passenger journeys throughout its life, though the Great Eastern briefly provided a through coach from Liverpool Street, slipped at Bentley and attached to the branch train, during 1876/77. Bus competition undermined the passenger service during the 1920s and this ended in 1932, though occasional excursions ran over the line into the British Railways period. Goods continued until 19 April 1965, sustained by the town's mills and maltings and latterly by horticulture and soft-fruit growing.

Shelford — Haverhill — Sudbury *

Passenger service withdrawn	6 March 1967	*Stations closed*	*Date of closure*
Distance	31 ¼ miles	Glemsford	6 March 1967
Company	Colchester, Stour Valley, Sudbury & Halstead Railway	Long Melford	6 March 1967
		Sudbury (first station)	9 August 1865

Stations closed	*Date of closure*
Haverhill	6 March 1967
Stoke	6 March 1967
Clare	6 March 1967
Cavendish	6 March 1967

* Closed passenger stations on this line that were in Cambridgeshire were Pampisford and Linton; the closed stations in Essex were Bartlow and Sturmer.

Haverhill Station.

Clare Station, *c*.1907.

The Stour Valley line was a cross-country route linking Cambridge to Colchester and serving a series of textile-making towns along the way. Samuel Courtauld set up his textile business in the area, later to grow into the multi-national company bearing his name, while Gainsborough and Constable both painted there. The railway, which departed from the main line to Liverpool Street at Shelford was typical of many of the cross-country lines built in the nineteenth century all over Britain – predominantly single-track, but capable of handling a significant volume of traffic and offering a diversionary route for main-line trains when required. Originally independent, the company was absorbed into the Great Eastern in August 1862.

Cavendish Station.

C·VE·DISH SUFFOLK Nº 35

At three points the line made junctions with branches. The route from Bartlow served Saffron Walden and joined the Cambridge–Liverpool Street main line at Audley End, while at Haverhill, and again beyond Sudbury at Chappel & Wakes Colne, connection was made with both ends of the independent Colne Valley & Halstead Railway, which largely duplicated that section of the Stour Valley line from across the county boundary in Essex.

The original single line was laid on a formation built to carry double track if required, though this was never in the event provided. Even so, the route was capable of running all but the largest of locomotives and served as a valuable alternative route east of Cambridge, either to Ipswich or to Essex coastal resorts like Clacton.

However, the existence of such a duplicate route defied the nostrums of the Beeching Report of 1963 and the line closed between Shelford and Sudbury to goods from 31 October 1966 and completely on 6 March the following year. The section from Sudbury to Marks Tey on the Colchester–Liverpool Street main line remains open.

Stations closed on lines still open to passengers
Ipswich — Beccles — Lowestoft

Original owning company East Suffolk Railway

Stations closed	*Date*
Bealings	17 September 1956
Melton *	2 May 1955

Stations closed	*Date*
Halesworth (first station)	1858 (exact date uncertain)

* Reopened 3 September 1984.

Melton Station.

Melton Station.

Ipswich — Bury St Edmunds

Original owning company	Ipswich & Bury St Edmunds

Stations closed	Date
Bramford (first station)	1912 (exact date uncertain)
Bramford (second station)	2 May 1955
Claydon	17 June 1963
Needham **	2 January 1967

Stations closed	Date
Haughley *	2 January 1967
Haughley Road	4 July 1849

* Renamed Haughley Junction in 1849, then Haughley Road in 1866, and then Haughley in 1890. It was known as Haughley West between 1923 and 1932.
** Reopened as Needham Market on 6 December 1971.

Claydon Station, *c.*1911.

G.E.R. STATION, CLAYDON. No.5.

Ipswich — Bury St Edmunds

Haughley — Norwich

Original owning company   Eastern Union Railway

Stations closed	*Date*
Finningham	7 November 1966
Mellis	7 November 1966

* Closed passenger stations on this line that were in Norfolk were Burston, Tivetshall, Forncett, Flordon, Swainsthorpe and Trowse.

Mellis Station.

The southbound platform at
Mellis, 9 September 1971.

Ipswich — Felixstowe

Original owning company	Felixstowe Railway & Pier Company

Stations closed	Date
Felixstowe Railway & Pier	1879 (exact date uncertain)
Orwell	15 June 1959
Felixstowe Beach	11 September 1967
Felixstowe Pier	2 July 1951

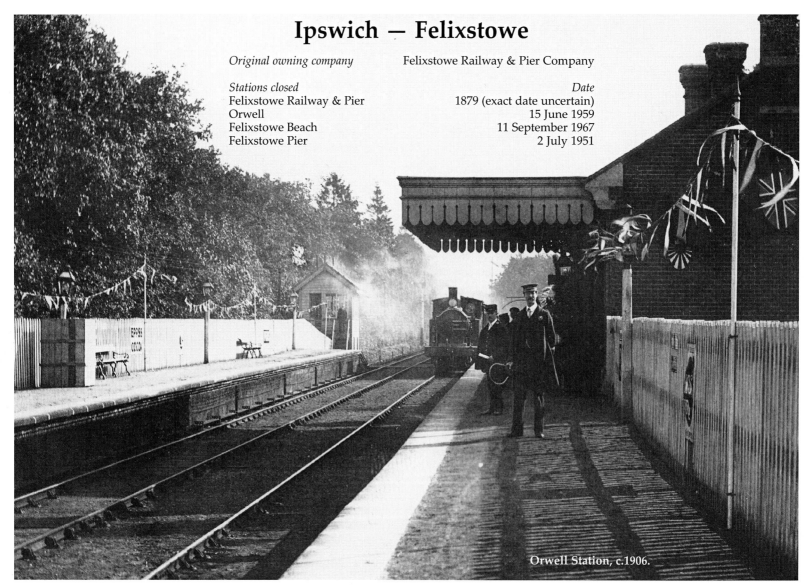

Orwell Station, c.1906.

Felixstowe Beach Station, looking towards the pier, 14 May 1956.

Newmarket — Bury St Edmunds

Original owning company   Newmarket Railway

Stations closed	*Date*
Higham	2 January 1967
Saxham & Risby *	2 January 1967

* Originally named Saxham but date of name change is unknown.

Higham Station.